How to be Debt Free

A proven strategy to take control of your financial freedom by getting rid of debt, loans, student loans repayment, credit card debt, mortgages and more

Volume 1

By

Income Mastery

TABLE OF CONTENTS

INTRODUCTION

"It's impossible to grow and prosper without making more investment."

MBA Managerial Encyclopedia

Have you ever wondered what the real concept of debt is?

Today, many people live in what is known as "the uncertainty of money"; the poor and middle class lived under certain rules of money and, although it is regrettable to say so, currently it is like that. After the uncertainty of what may happen, people are acting and living financially according to the old rule of "study an important career, work hard to earn a good salary, save money and spend it". Apart from the fact that this system does not currently work, the calmness behind the lack of progress has led new generations to save incompetently, people are sitting on a sack of money while they think they are saving it for their benefit or waiting for the situation they are living in now to stabilize, and on the other hand there are those who are "saving to spend later" without understanding that savings lose value, especially when inflation comes and grows faster than interest paid on savings accounts.

If we analyze this last point with a little discretion and attention, we might ask ourselves: So, is there some benefit in credit cards, bank credits and many other loans? The answer is yes, but only if you handle money with financial intelligence.

All this time we have been led to believe that this is the right way to do things, get a good job, be promoted, obtain a credit for a house and a car, buy "toys and whims" in installments or by bank financing, pay the minimum of credit cards to make you pay more money of the month or simply not get into debt with anything, because money is not good and "rich people do not have debts", but in reality it is not like that.

The way we invest and spend our money has a lot to do with the way we live and see the world, it even has to do with the way we perceive and project ourselves into the future. It is important to emphasize that although the technique of "working for something I want until I get it" does work, the results are short term and many times the cons are much more than we think; like how not to be comfortable with your work, not get the full money, to have a bad work experience or simply, notice that the satisfaction for had obtained what you wanted did not last as long as you expected and, among so many other things we will be thinking and acting like poor people, even though our house is full of those small "sacrifices turned into successes".

For many years we have been taught that the right way to have money is not having debts or that rich people are rich because they do not have debt, but what would happen if you figured out that all this is a myth, that money and some credits are not bad and that there are good debts and bad debts. Would you begin to invest intelligently and acquire some debts with an investor's conscience and eyesight? If your answer is yes, the information found in this book will help you to clarify any doubts you may have about money, initiate a strategy that will bring you closer every day to your financial freedom and overcome bad debts and not to be afraid of the good ones, because a rich person never loses the opportunity to take calculated risks.

Before beginning this financial journey where you will eliminate myths, taboos and certain outdated concepts regarding money, debts and their variants, it is important that you know the meaning of some key terms that will facilitate you the reading and understanding of this book.

Money: A mean of exchange, usually in the form of banknotes and coins, which is accepted by a company as payment of goods, services and all kinds of obligations. Its etymological origin leads us to the Latin word *denarius*, which was the name of the currency used by the Romans. *-Definition (website)*

Passive Income: Income generated without having to work for them, for example, income generated by real estate for rent, for businesses where we do not have to be present, or for paper assets such as stocks or bonds.
-Robert Kiyosaki

Earned Income: Income generated when we work for them, for example, by having a job, or a business that depends on our physical presence.
-Robert Kiyosaki

Assets: Anything that generates passive income for us, that is, anything that generates a cash flow for us, for example, a property in rent, a business where we don't have to be present, or a portfolio of shares.
-Robert Kiyosaki

Passive: Everything that generates expenses or makes us lose money.
-Robert Kiyosaki

Cash flow quadrant: A quadrant that shows four different types of people according to the income they earn; they can be: employee (E), self-employed (A), business owner or entrepreneur (D), and investor (I).
-Robert Kiyosaki

Leverage: That which allows us to make money significantly; there can be asset leverage, labor leverage, and financial leverage.
-Robert Kiyosaki

Money Speed: The speed at which money invested in one asset is recouped and then invested in another.
-Robert Kiyosaki

Loan: At the financial level, it is money that is requested or requested in a bank or similar entity. When you buy it, you have to repay it with interest.
-Definition (website)

Bad Debt: Debt that we pay.
-Robert Kiyosaki

Good Debt: Debt that someone else pays for us, for example, for a rental property, the bank gives us the loan, but our tenant pays for it.
-Robert Kiyosaki

Credit Bureau: is a private, non-governmental company that receives information from banks and financial institutions that grant loans to a natural or legal person. This information is stored in a credit history under the name of the person who requested it and in this way information is collected on each credit you acquire, its payments and debts.
-Iofacturo.mx (website)

Financial intelligence: That part of our intelligence we use to solve money problems is simply to have more options.
-Robert Kiyosaki

Financial freedom: A financial concept defined as the ability to stop working and continue generating income without the person's physical presence, and to obtain freedom of time, freedom of movement, and freedom of decision, basically achieved when your passive income (income that does not depend on your job) is greater than your expenses.

-Robert Kiyosaki and Camilo Cruz

"Financial education nurtures financial intelligence that leads to financial freedom."

Book Rich Father Poor Father, Robert Kiyosaki

MONEY CALLS MONEY

There are multiple beliefs about money, some managed by poor minds (intelligent, studied people who sell their time in exchange for money to acquire liabilities that look like assets) and others by wealthy minds (people who are financially educated, are not afraid to take risks, see opportunities in debt and are always looking for ways to invest in assets). It remains for us to know which to follow, the point now is to know how to differentiate which is a limiting belief in front of money and abundance and which is not.

T. Harv Eker says that we have a relationship with money that is formed many times from 0 to 7 years at an early age or later when we have a very specific situation in our money-related lives.

To determine the status of our relationship to money, it is best to carefully evaluate our thoughts and how we manage our income and expenses. This exercise will allow us to know our thought patterns, so that once we become aware of them, we can work on them.

This means that our relationship with money is influenced by everything we saw, heard and felt that it had a strong emotional charge in our life, so if you want to improve your relationship with money and make it flow abundantly in your life you must pay attention and work on a new schedule. To do this, the first thing we must do is to identify our limiting beliefs and then devote ourselves to finding examples of people who have money and who are extraordinary.

Some of the limiting beliefs we've grown up with can be:

1. If I have money, I'm gonna change and my family's gonna walk away.
2. If I have money, people don't really love me.
3. If I have money, I'm less spiritual.
4. Money connects with unhappiness and loneliness.
5. Money doesn't buy happiness.
6. The rich were born rich or they're lucky and I'm not.
7. It is better to work for something safe and a good salary than to take risks in the unknown.
8. Having a lot of material things makes me more important, no matter how I acquired them.
9. It is better never to get into debt before falling into a credit bureau.
10. "I prefer to be poor but honest," which in my opinion is the worst of all the previous ones, it's as if that means that having money can't be synonymous with honest and honest with the way we earn money, and basically translates into "I don't deserve it".

Definitely, our relationship with money and the way it flows and influences our lives and our pockets has a lot to do with reflecting what we think, feel and say about it.

Believing firmly in a universe of abundance and that we are the reflection of our thoughts and feelings, being then creators of our realities, is one of the first steps to attract money in a positive way in our lives and lead us towards the path of financial freedom.

Congruent with the steps to follow, once we recognize our limiting beliefs, organize and visualize our income and expenditures, and are willing to attract money, we begin with the part of following the people who are in the place where I want to go, from level one "I am able to get out of my debts and transform" to the maximum level "No matter if I work or not, money works for me constantly".

Tatiana Arias, one of the personalities who has influenced me the most in the way through financial education, is an enterprising businesswoman who has understood very well how the energy of money works and honors its concept, after having lived the maximum profit in salary, then the total bankruptcy, and emerge victorious and improved from this, tells us that the first thing we must understand is that without any doubt, money is energy and we can handle it in our lives as easily as we can block its arrival with our infinite limiting beliefs; also tells us that none of these beliefs are true, thinking that our happiness will depend only on the amount of money we have in our bank account is one of the main blocks to achieving financial success.

"Money is neither good nor bad, money is an amplifier, it is a mean that allows us to make exchanges for the things we want at this moment, whether goods or services."

When we understand the concept of money in this way and remove all negative emotions from money and see it simply as the resource we can use to help many people, it then becomes a very powerful tool.

At this point, we can then say that money is neither good nor bad, but the way we see, handle and use money can be catalogued in this way, according to the consequences and benefits of our actions with respect to our profits. For this reason, Robert Kiyosaki states that one of the correct ways to attract money is to educate ourselves financially, knowing the laws of the place where we are investing or managing a business to understand what advantages we have in front of a demand and also expand the panorama of possibilities and see investments where no one else (or very few) can see them. But the only way to get there is not by working for money, but for the love you put in whatever you do and for what you want to achieve, making mistakes as many times as necessary, and learning everything from sales and marketing to accounting and law.

The world today is in a serious financial crisis because the way our grandparents and parents were educated about money, how to receive it, manage it, and accept it is behind us. The current education system is completely out of date with respect to the new economy and the monitoring of inflation levels. People are still educated only to work, to get a good salary, to buy a house and to support their family, but only those who understand the true value and meaning of money come out ahead because of that, the rich are getting richer and the poor are even poorer, leaving behind the middle class which, depending on how things go, can become extinct at any moment and be "on the side of the rich or on the side of the poor".

Robert Kiyosaki and Donald Trump have noted this worrying situation and in consideration have written a book called "we want you to be rich" to initiate the process of financial education in the citizens of the United States of America and for those who are willing and interested in following the recommendations of this book and live in other countries of the world.

In this book, Robert and Trump comment with concern that the rich who want to improve things only donate money to the causes they believe in. But they in addition to money for foundations and a percentage of the profits from this book for institutions that teach financial education, give their time teaching and educating through their experience.

Trump and Kiyosaki in this book mention that there are three kinds of financial advice: for the poor, for the middle class, and for the rich. The financial advice for the poor is: "that the government will take care of them". The poor have social security and Medicare. The financial advice for the middle class is: get a job, work hard, spend as little as possible, save, invest for the future in investment funds and diversify. Most middle-class people are passive investors: investors who work and invest so as not to lose. The rich are active investors, who work and invest to earn. This book will teach you to be an active investor, to develop your resources to live a wonderful life working and investing to earn.

Knowing this, it is very important that we understand that the only thing that money cannot solve is poverty, simply because of the lack about financial education. Trying to solve our poverty problems with money will only lead to an unhappy, unsatisfied or worse, poor life, because money without financial education does not eliminate poverty.

In order to initiate this transformation of thoughts it is important that we completely forget about deserving, to discard that "I deserve this or that" mentality because I am a high-ranking soldier, teacher, business owner, wage earner or simply poor. The most practical way to solve this problem of poor financial results, distance and low return on money, is to change our way of thinking, start seeing the world and think like rich and not like poor or middle class. Because if we continue waiting for the others with greater capacities and better rank that we take charge, we will obtain again and again the same result, because as a wise man once said "you will never obtain different results as long as you continue to act in the same way". If our view of the world and money does not change, we will eternally be part of a bankrupt society, with well-educated but economically unstable and insecure people.

LOANS, MYTHS AND TRUTHS BEHIND THEM

Albert Einstein once said, "I think it's crazy to keep sending our kids to school without teaching them about money.

Knowledge is power, the importance of studying and knowing financial education today, goes beyond adding, subtracting, multiplying and dividing, knowing accounting and business administration. It is essential to know in a conscious way the work of the numbers, the pros and cons of the debts, the myths and the truths regarding the loans and above all to learn how to generate business strategies that place us in the maximum financial level that is to be investors. As described by Robert Kiyosaki in his quadrant book on money flow. However, all the great businessmen and successful investors emphasize that it is fundamental and of vital importance to study history together with our financial training, because this is the "secret" formula of all the rich people so as not to make the same mistakes of past generations and even help us to foresee the future of all our investments. In addition, knowledge of history can be timely in understanding, interacting and deciding on world events, both politically and financially.

As the saying goes, "Those who do not learn from history are condemned to repeat it.

In the same order of ideas, John Naisbitt in his books, Megatrends, Megatrends 2.0 and 11 Mentalities to foresee the future, tells us about the importance of observation and historical knowledge of the country where we live, of finances, of the great business cases and above all the daily study of each political, social and financial event that surrounds us, because this is what will allow us to program our brain and train us to know the future events and thus be able to foresee and even save all our investments, and if it is the case, our own company.

John, in 11 Mentalities for Anticipating the Future, defines mentalities as:

"Mentalities are key principles or ideas that operate as fixed stars. Our mind is like a drifting ship lost in an ocean of information and clinging to fixed stars we orient ourselves. It is the mentalities that maintain our course and guide us so that we can arrive safely at our destination. A common purpose of the eleven mentalities presented in this book is not to get lost in that which is not essential, but instead to concentrate on the things that have and will have the most influence in our lives.

Therefore, it can be said that a trained mind is a mind that looks for opportunities and does not look for solutions to problems, because it knows that in every opportunity there is an implicit problem that it is capable of solving. But now, what about people who don't study at all about finance and history, and don't train their brains for business and looking for opportunities? Simple, they get into debt. These people tend to always resort to their credit cards for unnecessary expenses, they buy liabilities with financing (which generates even more debts and losses by very high interests), they tend to work too much and they do not see the yield of their money because everything they produce goes in payments at the end of the month, plus the interests and the ants expenses; in addition to that the investments that they make with bank money tend to be "wrong" due to the lack of knowledge on how to multiply the money and to make that this works for them and not on the contrary. A seemingly adequate investment may be the purchase of a house, but what many do not know is that a house (with no lease opportunities or economic advantage) becomes a strong and extremely prolonged liability.

Although it is important to know that none of this is as alarming as it seems, we must consider the need (using this term in a slightly aggressive and categorical way) to have all the correct and exact information regarding the percentages of interest, loans, the credit bureau and of course the good and bad debts.

For this reason, it is important to begin to educate ourselves on all of the above issues, starting by denying some of those "truths" we hear in the street from inexperienced people (even from the same banks and financiers) regarding bank loans and debts.

We almost always make the mistake of listening to advice about financial care and investments, people have not achieved great things in their lives, or yet, they have not achieved "anything" at the financial level, and even, we usually listen to people of apparent success only by their constant flow of money without first asking ourselves if that space in which they are, is the place we want to reach. Among the things they usually tell us (and in many cases, unfortunately we often listen) these would be the most common:

- Bank loans are bad because you have to pay a lot of interest at a high price.

- All the interest, be it from a bank loan or financing in another entity, is too high and you will never be able to pay it off.

- The shorter the financing plan, the better because you won't lose money. It is important to clarify that all financing generates interest so it can be seen as a loss of money depending on the investment. Time has nothing to do with this, because the importance of what has been acquired and the profits it will generate generates greater weight.

- It's best to invest in a home of your own and pay off the credit as you can. This advice may be good depending on the level of inflation where we are, but if it is in a stable or moderately stable economy, it does not apply.

- No matter what you buy or if it is going to work for you, when you see that you can acquire it through financing or installments, do it, it will always be a good investment.

- The banks are the worst, if you don't pay the bank fees on time, you will fall into something they call the credit bureau and you will be completely banned from all the credits you want to opt for.

- Watch out for the credit bureau, that's part of the government and they know all about you!

- If you don't pay on time you will be seized and everything you have will be taken away until you are left on the street.

To quote John again to confirm all these previous points and the importance of knowing who to listen to and who not to listen, we must remember that: *"The things that we expect to happen always happen more slowly", which means* that if you hear these kinds of things and also follow them and believe them vehemently, they will end up happening in the same way. Although for the avoidance of doubt and misinformation it is better to continue reading because we will talk about the 7 myths of loans, we will explain what the credit bureau really is and even more we will talk about the two types of debt and when to acquire them.

It is understandable that we are terrified by the idea of getting into debt and thinking about going so far as not being able to make payments, as well as remembering our parents talking about the importance of saving, moderation and discipline. These are the necessary tools for professional improvement and for overcoming any unforeseen event in our daily lives. However, it is understandable that the country's economic situation, the high costs of daily living and unforeseen emergencies sometimes force us to look towards a path known as "the loan".

Now, to eliminate those fears and learn more about these credit issues and make better decisions in the future, let's start with the myths.

Myth 1: **The credit bureau belongs to the government and registers all debtors.**

The reality is that although the credit bureau shares our information with the banks, it is simply a private company that has nothing to do with the government and only handles accurate and concrete information of all people who have ever received a bank credit, which does not mean being on a blacklist, so the bureau is just a company that contains our banking data.

Myth 2: **If you're in the bureau, you can't get any credit.**

FALSE. This does not necessarily mean being exonerated from any credit just for having our banking and payment history, our credit information remains in the bureau database for 6 years. It is important to know that from the first moment we pay the credit, our names and financial behavior are completely recorded, because the bureau updates our information every 10 days and with this data the banks decide whether to grant us credit or not.

Myth 3: Paying for minimum payments will always be the best way

This really is one of the most common myths and greatest compliments of financial history; this is a bad financial habit because although in some cases it can be a great option (according to the business we are doing, the interest and the inflation rate), in other occasions it can be a "knife for our throat", since the profit trick is in the interests. Which means: the longer we take to pay, the more profit the bank will make.

Myth 4: Personal Loans are Extra Income

This is also false. A personal loan is a debt that must be repaid. This is the same mistake that is made when believing that credit cards are for enjoyment. All credits bear interest and are therefore responsible for payments. It is important to remember that all credits generate profits through interest.

Myth 5: Borrowing from friends or acquaintances is better than borrowing from the bank.

This is the main myth that we must remove from our head, first of all because it can bring us many family and financial problems. In addition, borrowing from our acquaintances may seem advantageous, but it really is if the amount is very low and we commit to pay on a timely date for both parties, allowing this to be short term or to one no longer than 3 months..

It is preferable that if we require a much larger loan, we apply to banks, cooperatives or other financial institutions, analyzing of course which offers us the best forms of payment and lower interest rates. If we don't have an income that generates a good ability to pay, then the best thing is not to get into debt because we could put all our reputation at risk and lose relationships with friends and family.

It is important to point out that the only advantage of borrowing from people close to you is that this loan, even if it is short term, may not result in interest losses. However, the best advice is simply not to get this type of loans - debts.

Myth 6: Any credit we get is because we can afford it.

This may be true and at the same time it may not be true, in fact it is a relative myth; indeed the entity makes a credit evaluation of our banking profile and history and verifies if we have the capacity to pay enough to charge us for the financial responsibility we are about to acquire, but this does not mean a guarantee of payment or loan.

Many economists suggest that when we want to get into debt, consider if this loan can be worth it, that is to say that it is a good debt, of those that are taken as an investment that generates great benefits in the future. and that although they offer us more than we have asked for. To do this, we must consider our current situation and be honest about whether or not we will be able to acquire such a debt. It is good to remember that the less we get into debt and the less time we make payments, the better for our pockets and our peace of mind.

Myth 7: If you don't pay, your house will be taken away and collectors will not stop calling you.

It is true that all finance companies have a collection office, and that their function is to be persistent at the time of collection, so much so that sometimes they can get to the point of falling into harassment. However, there are specialized entities that are responsible for publishing the guidelines of conduct for the collection departments of companies and thus prevent them from making calls at inappropriate times or take actions that invade our privacy.

Although it's good to know that the best way to avoid debt collectors is to pay on time and keep all our credit payments current. Besides, this exonerates us from losing what we've mortgaged.

At this point it is good to mention the myth about shipments. Normally we tend to fall into this myth for lack of knowledge. No one can take our home or any other property without us having put it as a guarantee, unless we have acquired a mortgage loan. But usually the companies that grant personal loans ask for a guarantee or a guarantee that depending on the moment can be from a telephone, a tv or any electrical appliance, to a house or a car.

On the other hand, there are some financial entities that can offer you the credits without the need to present a guarantee, simply because we have a good credit history.

It should be noted that there are companies that do not ask for any kind of collateral and usually make personal loans with much lower interest rates compared to the rest. This is the case of some companies that lend money through the web, that is to say, that the personal credits are by Internet and in exchange you only have to have a good financial history.

In the same order of ideas, knowing these myths about loans, understanding the meaning of money and cutting with so many taboos, it is important to consider some recommendations on the subject already exposed.

Recommendations

- Putting together a budget of fixed monthly spending and secure cash inflows will help us keep our accounts in order and know how much money we can and can't count on daily. In order to keep this budget the first step is to know what is the amount of fixed monthly money we receive, then, the best thing we can do is to domicile the payments of services such as electricity, water telephone, among others, directly to our, knowing what is the minimum monthly overhead of services, but calculating it to the maximum to foresee and not have loss of money or negative numbers at the time of drawing accounts.

- Another important recommendation for not acquiring more unpayable debts is not to fill us with interests that exceed (between the sum of all) more than 30% of our monthly earnings, because only in this way will you be able to take a better control of the surplus of money for necessary basic expenses.

- Forget about the ant expenses, those that take away our money for unnecessary and capricious purchases, that look small in amounts but at the end of the month they add a considerable number for effects of our expenses and our savings.

- Last but not least, remember to prioritize your debts and fixed expenses and forget about the idea that credit cards are cash because they don't, they generate interest debts and add information to your credit history.

Very well, now that we know all these myths, we can be more aware when acquiring a bank loan or debt, but before assuming the position of financial leaders and completely refusing to assume any debt (because this position is also valid and very accurate) we must know the difference between a good debt and a bad debt.

When does it make sense to get into debt?

If our goal is to achieve financial freedom, it is important to know that there are debts that will help to achieve that goal and others that will definitely keep us away from it. If you continue to read with enthusiasm, it's because this topic is definitely for you. In this section we'll look at what all this is about good debts, something we've thought doesn't exist and probably just read in this book.

When we talk about debts we can distinguish two types, good debts and bad debts, knowing how to recognize them will make us richer, but if we are not yet able to identify the differences between the two, we can dangerously get stuck for a long time in the rat's career, we and our constant flow of money will go from profits and positive interests, to the misleading state of the rat's career, a term that Robert Kiyosaki explains and defines as the state in which we work only to get out of debt and get more and more credit. This will make us fall into an eternal cycle of collecting - paying - acquiring new debt, making it much more difficult to achieve the financial freedom we so long for.

Now, if our goal is not to reach the life of the much mentioned Robert Kiyosaki and Donald Trump, life with financial freedom, but the reach of static capital (investment in saleable movable goods such as televisions, appliances, sofa games, sound equipment, among others) this cycle or this race of the rat may be an option or a valid game to achieve that goal.

At this point you will surely ask yourself, then what are the good debts and the bad debts? Well, bad debts are all those that we acquire and that can only benefit a bank or anyone who has been the entity that granted us the loan and that in our personal balance (that we have done previously to know our inputs and outputs) becomes a liability that constantly generates expenses and very high interest to pay (more than 30% of our fixed monthly income). Therefore, they become an expense that will come directly out of your pocket and that can only be paid by you with your fixed monthly income, and not with the gain received from the credit acquired.

A classic example of a bad debt is acquiring a good or a service from something we don't really need and which only responds to a whim or impulse of the moment, such as a new refrigerator or a larger television, even though the one we already have still works, or a three-week vacation for which we will be forced to pay very high interests for more than three months.

The fact of acquiring a bad debt, can reflect the lack of control and discipline that we have with our finances, in addition to little knowledge in financial education; these debts usually we acquire them in an unintelligent way and with very dangerous credit instruments such as lenders, credit cards, long-term financing, among others.

But on the other hand, there is the little-known world, or rather, only known to successful people, that is, those with education and financial intelligence; and it is the world or the reality of what they define as "good debts". These are all those debts that we acquire to generate assets that in turn generate even more assets, but this is only possible when we get into debt intelligently. That is to say, that we acquire active goods that generate a financial retribution, or more concretely, they produce money for us; as it can be the acquisition of a commercial premises, a property that generates profits for us (real estate that we can rent), a superior formation (because to educate us financially and of correct form will always be a good investment) or acquiring an antiquity that is revalued with the time by its historical importance. For this last point it is important to know about history in order to avoid acquiring products badly called antiques, which instead of being revalued suffer depreciation, that is to say, they lose their economic value.

A very clear example, given by Robert Kiyosaki, is investment in real estate. If a bank offers us a credit of $500,000, we can take that credit and with the choice of two options, we could get the purchase of a property at $100,000 or less, the remaining money returned to the bank as immediate payment of the credit, this property put it into rent which can be an approximate of $1200 less taxes, and with this rent pay the outstanding installments of the remaining credit. Surely we will obtain a remaining profit of about 200$ net, 200 with which we do not count monthly as a constant income.

On the other hand, with the credit we could buy 5 properties of 100.000$ and rent them; the quotas of the credit would be approximately of 5000$ monthly, if each lease produces us an income of 1200$ deducting taxes, we will obtain 6000$ net, with which we will be able to pay the monthly quota of the bank and in addition we would have an asset of 1000$ monthly that increases when finishing paying the credit. Precisely this is what is known as intelligently managing money, acquiring good debts, generating constant assets and definitely making money work for us, but we can only see this as an investment opportunity when we have financial intelligence.

HOW TO GET OUT OF DEBT
AND START EARNING

If

you want to stop being poor and start living a rich and millionaire life, without being a victim of global changes, it is important that you develop the most important thing you have with you, YOUR MIND, because your financial education is the main engine for your economic growth.

Remember that the winners have high aspirations, enthusiasm and short, medium and long term plans. Perhaps your ideas may seem out of touch with reality, but it all starts with a dream and a crazy idea, just pay attention to the details and concentrate on seeing which can lead you to make your dreams come true. Donald Trump said one day at a meeting with important businessmen: "I invest to win, don't you?" and only those who had a real financial education felt identified with this, because only winners invest to win, others invest not to lose.

The great business leaders and investors, recommend people who want to live like them, begin to assume successful and be very stubborn to the point of achieving all the objectives. Positive thinking and constancy work and have a lot of power, being a winner requires that kind of power, whether you are extrovert or introverted because shyness here has little to do with it.

Ignorance is very costly, much more so than education, and that includes financial education. The fear of the unknown often causes us to lose millionaire opportunities, do not allow that to steal your aspirations and financial well-being preventing you from achieving the life of the great ones. Power over our emotions and thoughts is one of our greatest strengths and is an important key to success. Being positive and focusing on your financial education can help you overcome difficult situations and determine those people who just want you to feel unable to take advantage of you.

Learn about money, make mistakes, educate yourself and work harder every day until you get the money to work for you, that's the key to successful investments.

Well, now that we have various insights into the key concepts of how the energy of money works, how we can handle it intelligently and what the steps to follow and the way of thinking of a winner are, it is important to also understand how we can get out of our debts quickly and without more complication than generating a good plan of action.

The best way to start is without a doubt, creating the habit of keeping a monthly balance of all our income and expenses, this will allow us to understand more accurately what we are spending our money on and how we are managing it, if it is good or if we are really wasting it. This is important because many times we are not aware of why we get into debt, what we spend the money on or what we invest it in, and many times we do not know if it is really necessary for our financial growth that investment or expense we are thinking of making and we end up with an immense list of all the accounts payable that in time will only generate a great headache, frustration and even much disillusionment and demotivation.

For all this there is a simple solution, if we begin to create the habit of analyzing our expenses in detail, we will be able to know with greater clarity which are really important and necessary and which are not, in such a way we will be much more intelligent at the moment of acquiring our debts and from the first instant we will generate our action plan to leave them as soon as possible and without any type of complications.

There are various exercises and ways to keep our financial control, this practical exercise that you will read below, will offer you a method that consists of only four simple steps to get out easily and quickly of all the debts you may have and will allow you to have absolute control of your money and even the awareness of spending (in what to spend and what not to do) that few have.

STEP 1

IDENTIFY WHERE YOU ARE RIGHT NOW

The first step is as simple as identifying where you are, a question that seems to be very simple but takes an important and profound work of analysis and internalization.

Where are you today? It is of the utmost importance that we respond clearly and honestly to where we are financially at the moment, because this is what will push us to where we would like to be, and in turn will allow us to be clear about what we must do to get there. It is therefore a matter of vital importance.

Sitting down, calculating and getting the total figure of our debt is step 1.1. It is important to clarify that after knowing this sum and see if we have or not the money to get out of it soon is something that can generate a lot of stress, but it is necessary that you take this first step as the beginning to reach the trip of your dreams, or better still to reach your financial tranquility. In the end this process will become a positive consequence of having performed this exercise.

All this is necessary because in order to know how to get out of all our debts, the first thing we must do is make an inventory of how much money we owe, to whom and the reason why we owe it, that is, what we spend it on.

To do this, we will make a table of several columns in an Excel or Word file or in a notebook that we will use to control our finances, and we will classify them in the following way:

First column identifies who you owe (name of subject or store).

Second column, what is the total sum of the debt to each name or invoice mentioned above, if there are several invoices specify them and add them all, and then place the final amount obtained (it is important to place the items on which we spent that money).

Third column, place what is the total sum of interest generated by debts (this is debts with interest such as loans or credit cards, bank loans, financed purchases, etc.).

Fourth column, establishes a minimum monthly payment and if you owe to friends or colleagues, establishes a payment quota to each one proposing them to return their money even if it is in parts. Add up all these payments and establish your total minimum monthly payment, to propose this goal to you on a monthly basis and take it out of the money you have available for food and other expenses. If, on the other hand, you receive money fortnightly or weekly, you can adapt those minimum payments to weeks or fortnights so that you can get out of these debts even faster.

STEP 2

USE THE "SNOWBALL DEBT METHOD"

The snowball debt method is a strategy proposed by Dave Ramsey, author of "The Total Transformation of Your Money", and is performed to eliminate personal debts that we have acquired through credit cards, mortgages and others; this method basically consists of paying first the lowest debt, and making minimum payments to the other larger debts. So, once you have paid that first debt (the smallest and least expensive), you will concentrate on the next smaller debt, and so on until you reach the largest or even total payment of all.

According to Dave Ramsey, this strategy is used in the following way: if, for example you have a $100,000 mortgage, you have an additional $15,000 personal loan, you also have 1.200 dollars of expenses on one credit card and $500 of expenses on another credit card and, besides you have expenses of a receipt or two pending of about $100 in the library or gym or some classes that you take, then you should concentrate on paying off first that debt of $100, also making minimum payment contributions to the rest of your debts (the minimum payment for debts and in general that you determined in step 1). After you have paid off this first debt in full, you should concentrate on paying off the next smaller debt, in this case, the $500 you have on one of your credit cards.

Some accountants and economists think that this system goes totally against financial logic, because any of them will tell you to pay first, and as soon as possible, that debt that regardless of whether the amount is high or low, generates or charges you higher interest because "this way the debt will grow less over time and you can use your money more efficiently". Although this is true in some way and may work, this snowball method doesn't tell you to stop paying the minimum of other debts, for this reason it makes it efficient because what is really behind the strategy has very little to do with efficiency and much more to do with some psychological principles that modify human behavior. This is why the snowball tends to work better than any other strategy for many people.

Why is that? I don't know. Very simply, by paying first or setting aside every penny of dollar you have available to face the smallest debt or lower cost, you can cross that amount relatively quickly from your list of debts, thus becoming more effective to pay the next debt that will be the next lower figure and thus, to get those quick small victories your motivation will increase. This is very important because if you worry too much (to the point of stress and emotional chaos) about the amount of money to be paid and focus first on the largest debts, it will be much easier for you to feel powerless in the face of the large amount of accumulated debt. But by facing the smallest debts until you eliminate them soon from your list, you will begin to win the battle and you will realize that you are capable of winning this financial war.

So, this strategy works the motivation, allowing to see that from the economic organization and establishing a margin of weekly, monthly or fortnightly expenses, you will be able to put an end to that list of accounts payable. It is often better to follow human nature than certain numerical logics (even if they work), but of course this method works better with certain types of people. As any other psychological and cognitive method works, although it will never be too much to know other alternatives.

Don't feel overwhelmed when you take out the structure of steps 1 and 2, this process is very similar to any other that can be spent in an environment of personal productivity to the point where you can get to the point where the mountain called "debts" (too many tasks and projects pending completion) is so overwhelming that you may feel lost, unfocused or hopeless.

So, in that case, it's possible that the snowball approach can help you find the motivation you need to get everything back in order. Don't forget that every time you pay and you have already solved your obligatory daily affairs, you dedicate yourself then to face that small task owed and you begin to cross out, cross out and cross out all the negative numbers that were already paid.

Remember to start from the smallest, because if you're faced with a giant and a little intimidating task you'll probably be scared, but if you reduce the size of the problem and make it small enough, you'll be able to win battles faster and faster. And so, once you've taken full control of your financial life, you'll feel motivated enough to start thinking with a different mathematical logic and much more careful and optimal. In this way it will be easy for you to face any economic decision, to act with efficiency and common sense.

Tatiana Arias and many other people have used this method and have validated it, after having seen good results, and recommend another plus for this strategy that can also work and is that once you have paid the smaller debts, then put the focus on paying that debt that generates higher interest, since that will now be the one that frees you more money when you pay it month after month. But in addition to choosing it and focusing on it, the advice is to pay a little more over the minimum payment whether it's $5, $10 or the amount of dollars that is within your range of possibilities and that eventually does not leave you short at the end of the month to pay other fixed monthly expenses.

Almost always in finance the habit is more important than the amount, that is why, in these cases debtors, if you want to get out as soon as possible from the accounts payable, it is extremely important to enter into a dynamic of paying a little more than the minimum each month.

There are still two more steps to go, but only by consistently applying these first two steps can I assure you that you will be able to get out of your debts very quickly and intelligently.

Remember that your attitude will depend on your motivation to follow the plan, and that only we have the ability to make this task easier and simpler if we have a mentality of focus, perseverance, positivism and of course courage and willingness to win.

ROCKY POWER

Although it may not seem like it, this is one of the most important steps to get out of debt, since it is the one that will keep us focused on our goal, to leave the red numbers at zero.

Those who have seen Rocky's film may remember that some of the things that characterized this character were his perseverance and tenacity to achieve his goal, which was simply to go out to win, for this reason this step is called so, because like him we must take care of our attitude to the circumstances. Since, in order of accounts, it will be this one that determines the time that we will take to pay our debts according to the dates and goals that we set ourselves.

It is important to stop doubting our mind and ability to achieve things, because the right attitude of approach is what will lead us to understand how the energy of money works, how to stay free of debt and make peace with it, to begin to intelligently invest our capital.

STEP 4

POSITIVE MONEY

In this step is where we find the magic that will allow us to get out of debt without the need to earn more money than we already earned; of course, if you get the opportunity to increase your income is also good and important, but remember to start spending your money wisely because the more you earn, the more you spend.

The "positive money" step is a system of "financial happiness" created by Tatiana Arias, this system is based on working the abundance and all that money that is released or created to be available at the end of the month.

And how is that done? Well very simple, the first step to apply this method and get out of debt faster, is through the optimization of monthly fees for basic fixed monthly services such as cell phone, television, electricity, food purchases, among others.

It is important for you to be aware of several things such as: How many technological devices do you have in your home and office that you don't use and don't sell? All of that, instead of having him paralyzed there, can contribute to generating positive money for you.

Many times it is difficult to see this kind of thing as something that can bring us more money, because almost always we tend to feel attachment to these materials that came into our lives through much work effort and surely the first thing that comes to mind when you have to get out of debt is to believe that it is only possible if you earn much more money, and that really is not the case.

If you don't start changing your mentality or habits first, the moment you start earning more money, you'll also start spending a lot more and acquiring materially delinquent and leisure products that will generate more debt. That's why investing your time in trying to change your relationship with money is essential to start your journey and get out of debt, additionally it is just as important that you invest time in working the material detachment, getting to see that objects around you that you can sell because they have a lot of time without use and that their sale will also free you from a few debts and red figures on your list.

Once you change your relationship with money and consistently generate positive money, continually attracting money to you and now thinking much more intelligently financially, then it's time to start investing and making the money work for you and not you for it. Your job at that time will not be to think about how to pay debts when you earn more money, but on the contrary your mission will be to think with the money you earn TODAY, how you will organize your personal finances to begin to pay those debts of acquired liabilities and assume now good debts that generate assets.

Now that you know all the steps and your mind has greater financial education and winning investor mentality, remember to write your own script, that one where you draw your perfect life, then reproduce it and live as you want to do because that is freedom, that is power and that is definitely winning. Grant yourself the dream come true of financial freedom that will lead you to be who you really want to be and work just for the love of what you do and not for the need to generate maintenance money.

Take care, your mind is your most important asset and the main lever to take you to the place where you want to be, then you must be very careful and jealous with what you put it, with what you consume; because sometimes it is much more difficult to get rid of old thoughts and ideas that are already in our psyche than to learn something new and important.

Those cases of "luck" called in some cultures "leverage" can come in many forms, one of them can be your thought. All the successful people that exist in the world take care of their body in an intelligent way and above all they take care of their brain, not only through food but through thoughts, because they do not think about things like "I will never be able to do that", "this is too much for me" "I do not have the necessary money to achieve it" but on the contrary they program themselves looking for solutions and filling themselves with strategic thoughts like "How can I achieve it and what should I do? How can I face those risks and reduce them? How do I get the money I need?

It is important to be clear that life is full of risks and we don't have absolute control of all the things that can happen to us, no matter how much we like to think otherwise. But we do have the capacity to reduce risks and increase our growth and financial freedom through learning, the reasonable and reasoned decisions we make and, of course, our positive and persevering attitude towards situations. Many financially successful people like Donald Trump have achieved that freedom even though all odds were against them and they did it because they decided to take control of their destiny and refused to give up so easily.

Robert Kiyosaki and Donald Trump say, "*If you do the minimum, you'll get the minimum. In the end, your results won't be exceptional. To stand out, you must do what others are not willing to do.* You can make the most of your time and all the talents and potential you have and the place where you are now and where you want to go. You just have to get ready to do more. What you're willing to do is what determines how far you're going to go.

That's why it's important to control not only our income and expenses, and keep our debts badly paid, but also to educate yourself; for the more you learn, the more you'll realize how much you didn't know and the less time and business opportunities will go unnoticed in front of you.

The best and most important thing to achieve our financial freedom is that we learn to think for ourselves through constant financial education, trial and error, and perseverance, until we polish our own eagle's eye, rather than someone else who might not have good intentions doing it for us. Taking courses in accounting and business law is important for those who want to manage money intelligently and invest it to put it to work for themselves, no matter they do not have the plan to be accountants or lawyers, this will save them several years of "mistakes".

As Louis Pasteur said, "Chance favors prepared minds." But if, on the other hand, your goal is just to stay debt free and lead a quiet, uncomplicated life is fine, it's important as an adult to know what lifestyle you want. No one is good or bad, the question is that you start planning now what you want and materialize it before it is too late, especially if the main desire is to live like Queen Elizabeth and her relatives, then the suggestion is to start looking for that castle right now.

Life is too short not to dream of achieving that castle, or whatever aspect keeps for you your dream and need, but it is important not to forget that there are more important things than money, start investing in that which you love because love is the key to a life of health, wealth and happiness. It is much easier to be healthy if you are happy, it is much easier to be rich if you are happy and it is even easier to be happy if you love what you do.